GOOD VIBES

Easy Coloring Book for Adults Inspirational Quotes

THIS BOOK BELONG TO

____
____
____
____

THIS BOOK BELONG TO

ARE YOU READY

TAKE IT EASY

NOThiNG
WORTH
HAViNG
COMES
EASY

BE SO GOOD
THEY CAN'T
IGNORE YOU.
- STEVE MARTIN

DiE WiTH MEMORiES,
NOT DREAMS

DON'T WAIT;
THE TIME
WILL NEVER
BE JUST RIGHT

LET YOUR PAST
MAKE YOU BETTER
NOT BITTER

IF YOU WANT TO FLY, GIVE UP EVERYTHING THAT WEIGHS YOU DOWN

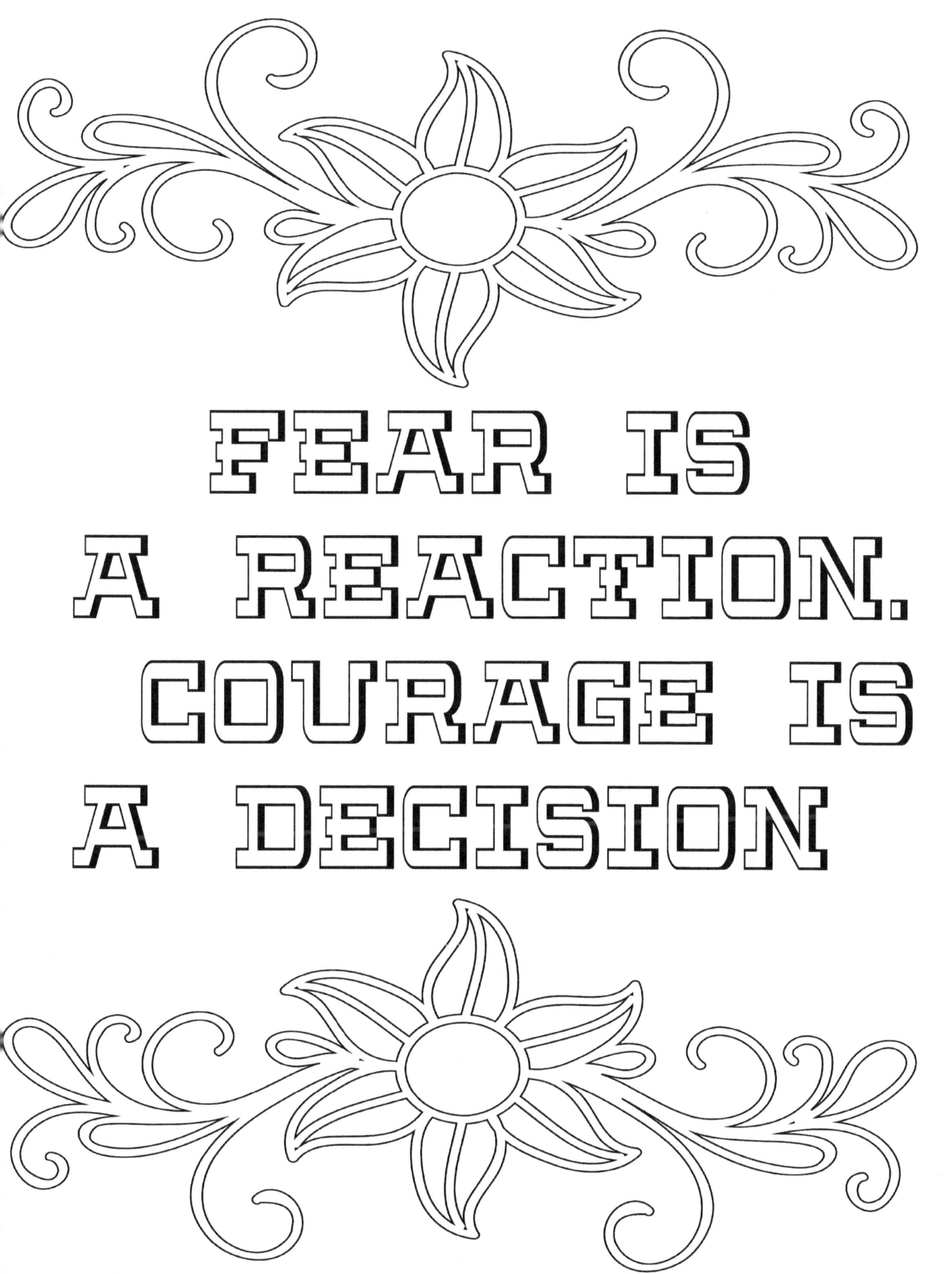

FEAR IS
A REACTION.
COURAGE IS
A DECISION

MY LIFE IS MY MESSAGE

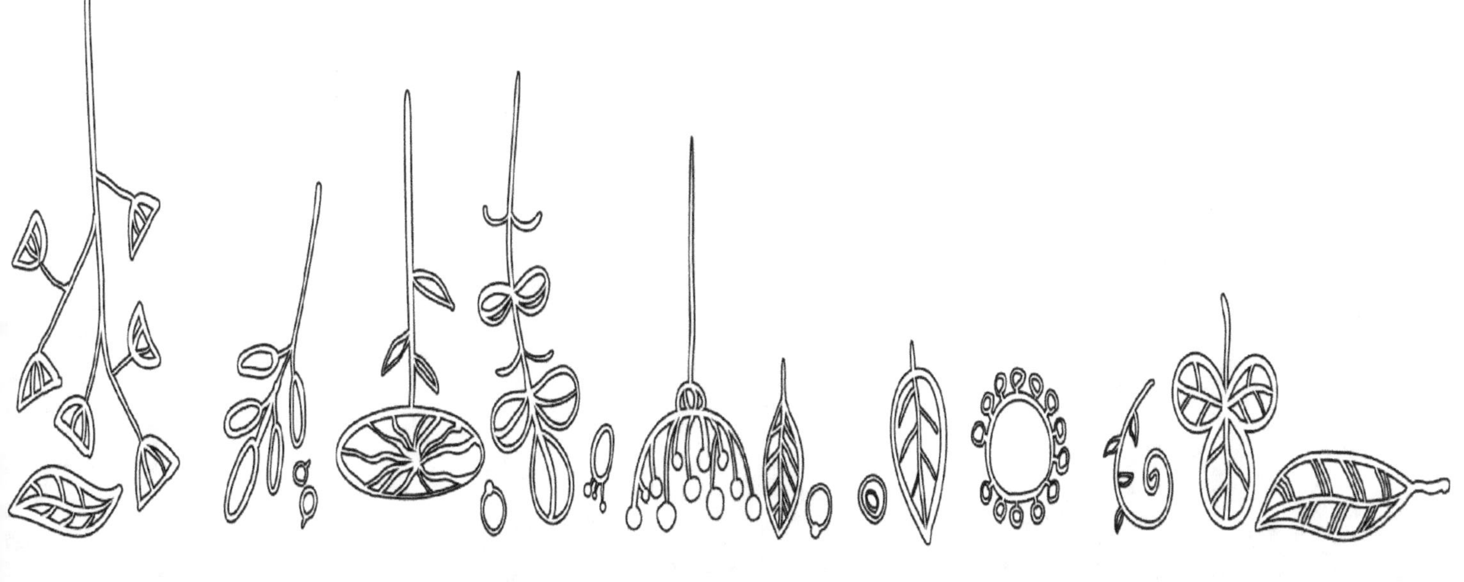

NO
GUTS,
NO
STORY

EITHER YOU
RUN
THE DAY,
OR THE
DAY
RUNS YOU

EVERY NOBLE
WORK IS
AT FIRST
IMPOSSIBLE

BE
YOUR
OWN
BOSS

IF YOU KNOW YOU CAN DO BETTER... THEN DO BETTER

WHAT HURTS US
IS WHAT HEALS US

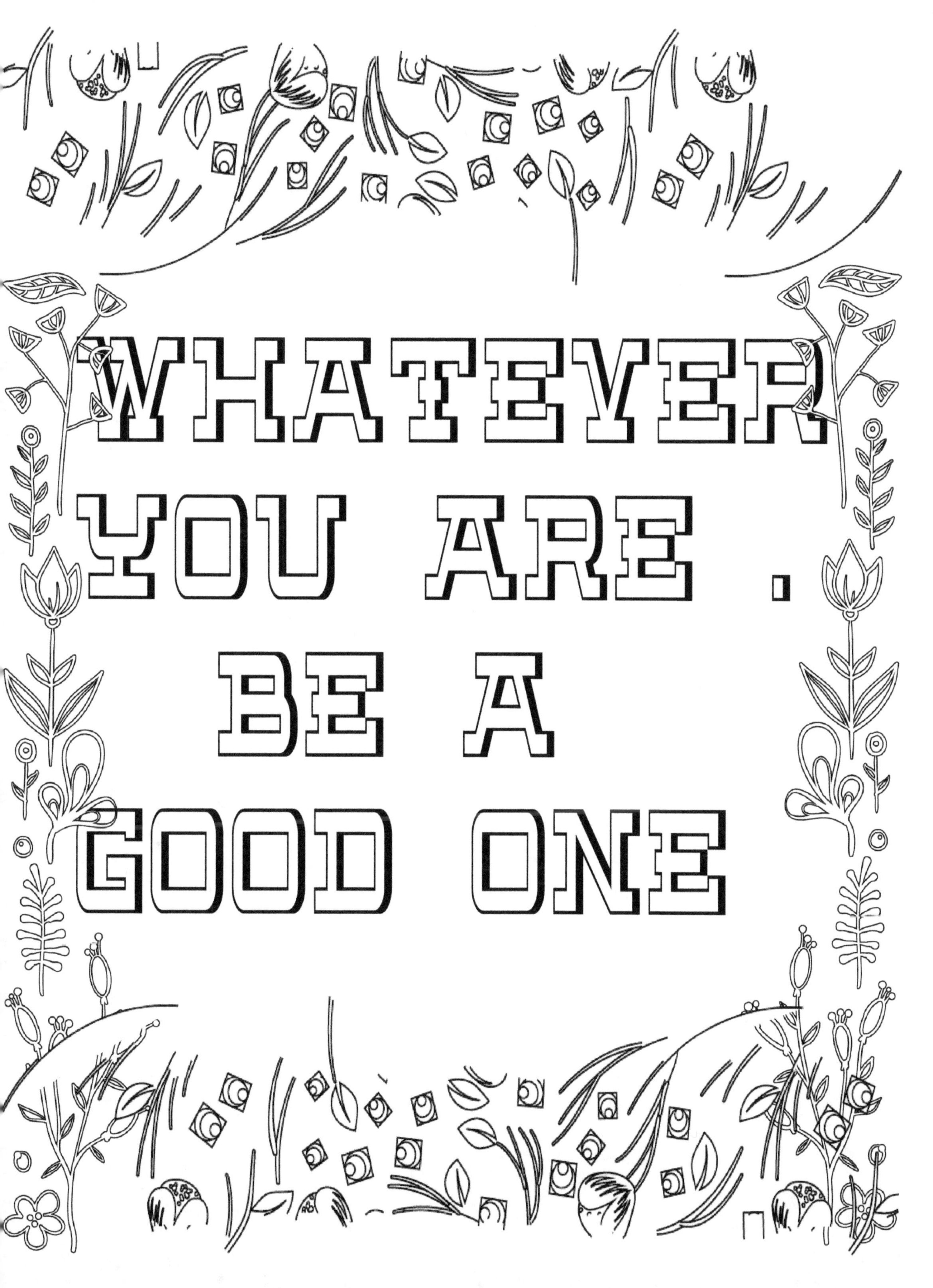

WHATEVER
YOU ARE .
BE A
GOOD ONE

ASPIRE TO
INSPIRE
BEFORE WE
EXPIRE

DON'T TELL PEOPLE
YOUR PLANS.
SHOW THEM
YOUR RESULTS

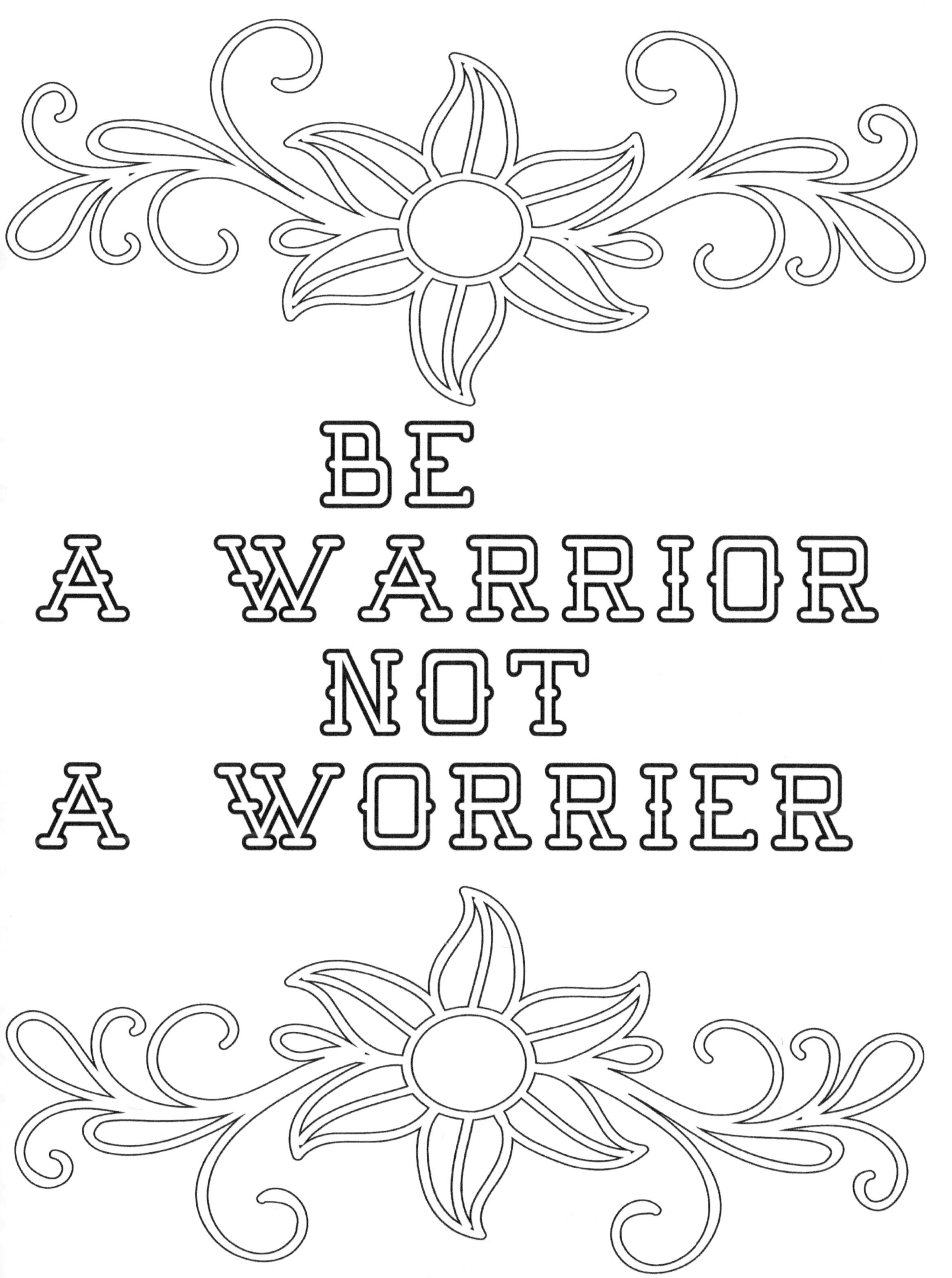
BE
A WARRIOR
NOT
A WORRIER

FEEL THE FEAR
AND
DO IT ANYWAY

WHAT CONSUMES YOUR MIND CONTROLS YOUR LIFE

DON'T JUST EXIST ,
LIVE

NEVER
STOP
DREAMING

Love more
Worry less

COLLECT MOMENTS ..
NOT THINGS

WORK HARD.
STAY HUMBLE

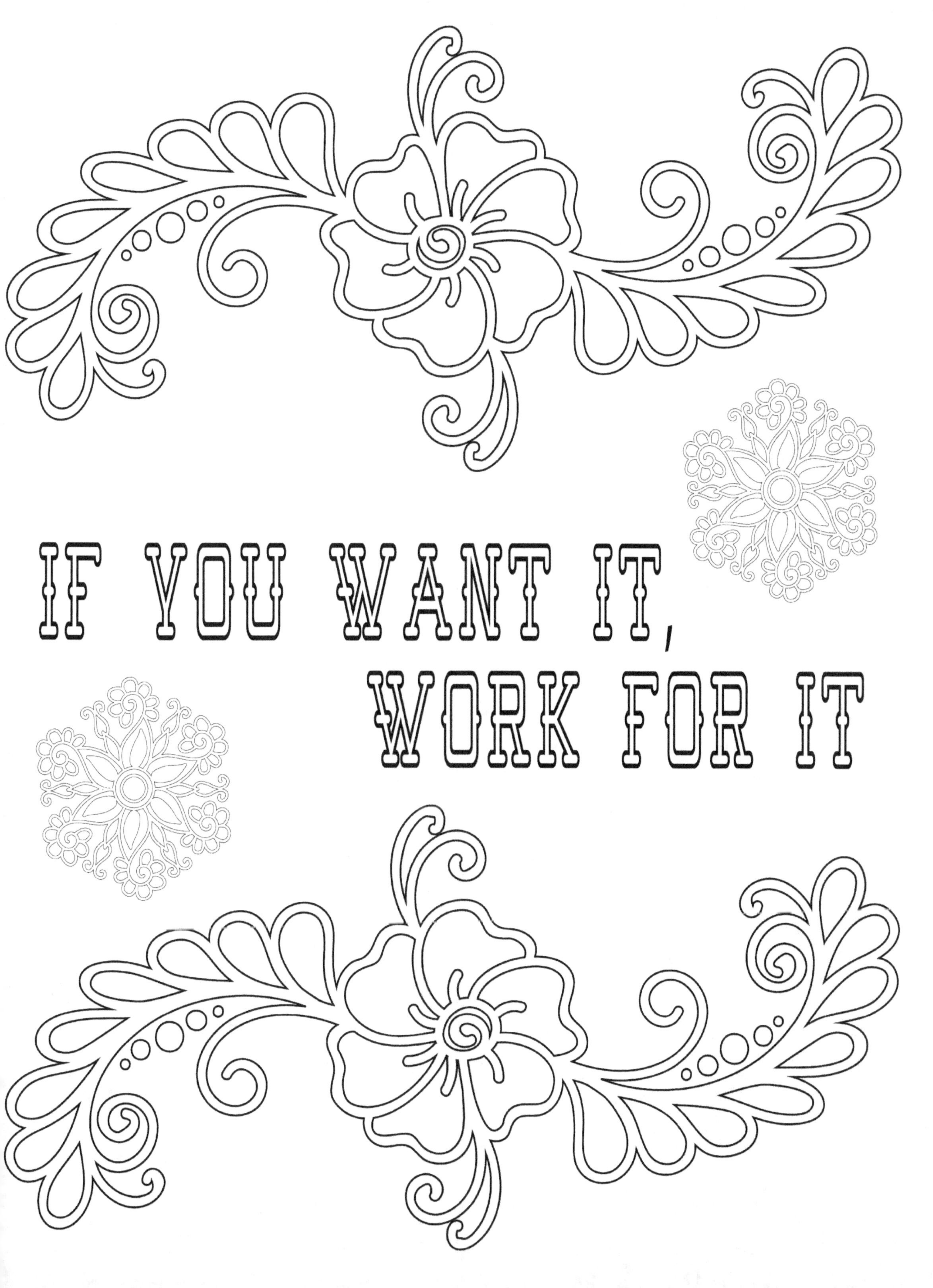

IF YOU WANT IT,
WORK FOR IT

DREAM BIG.
PRAY BIGGER

FALL SEVEN TIMES,
STAND UP EIGHT.
"Japanese Proverb"

HOPE YOU LIKE MY BOOK